Flute/Violin

An Easy Approach to Improvising in Funk, Soul, Lat... ...les

FREE to SOLO

Rob Hughes and Paul Harvey

www.schott-music.com

SCHOTT

Mainz · London · Berlin · Madrid · New York · Paris · Prague · Tokyo · Toronto
© 2011 SCHOTT MUSIC Ltd, London · Printed in Germany

Contents

About the authors

Rob Hughes is an experienced London-based musician and composer with an extensive list of live performances to his credit including: Gloria Gaynor, Mark Ronson, All Saints, Chuck Berry, ABC, Daniel Merriweather, Anastacia and Heather Small.
In 2006 Rob released his debut album *Butterfly* and a second album *The London Experiment* in 2010 (both as a solo artist). As well as performing, Rob has taught extensively for over 15 years.

For more info visit www.robhughesmusic.com

Paul Harvey is a guitarist and songwriter who works as a session musician. He has recorded and played live with various artists including: Prefab Sprout, Ellis Beggs and Howard, Tom Robinson, Then Jerico, Carol Decker (T'Pau), Thomas Dolby, Kool and the Gang, Bob Geldof, Kiki Dee, Cliff Richard, Boy George, Gary Numan, Andy Taylor (Duran Duran) and Brenda Edwards (X Factor). Paul is also in great demand as a London-based teacher.

ED 13373

British Library Cataloguing-in-Publication Data.
A catalogue record for this book is available from the British Library.
ISMN M-2201-3224-7
ISBN 978-1-84761-244-1

Project management, layout and copy editing by Scott Barnard for MusicPreparation (www.musicpreparation.co.uk)
Cover design and photography by www.adamhaystudio.com

Printed in Germany S&Co.8706

Welcome

This book has been designed to develop your capacity to improvise on contemporary tunes. Composed in contrasting styles, with an emphasis on having fun, the play-along backing tracks will inspire you to improvise with greater confidence, without having to worry about multiple scales – in essence you will be 'Free To Solo'.

How to use this book

Each of the 9 tunes has its own challenge and will improve your soloing skills by focusing on four areas:

Style & History This section will discuss the background and features of various genres, together with suggested listening. Styles covered include funk, folk, Motown, jazz, pop, reggae, ballads and Latin.

Harmony The idea is to solo freely whilst listening to the harmony on the audio tracks provided, without being constrained by too much jazz theory. The majority of the pieces have been designed to work with a single pentatonic or major scale. Chord symbols are included throughout for more advanced players.

Rhythm This section deals with how to play tricky rhythms as well as ideas about developing a solo from a rhythmic point-of-view.

Tips & Projects Here you are invited to take your study a little further. This will involve transcribing parts of the demonstrated solo, writing an alternative melody, more advanced harmonic ideas and guidance on solo structures.

Below is an explanation of the scales most frequently used in this book. It's a good idea to be familiar with them and be able to play them in a variety of keys.

Major pentatonic scale – Pentatonics consist of five notes: the root, 2nd, 3rd, 5th and 6th of the major scale.

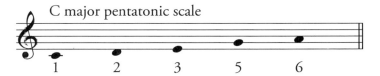

Minor pentatonic scale – this is also constructed from five notes, but they are slightly different from the major version. It uses the root, 3rd, 4th, 5th and 7th of the natural-minor scale. (Note the 3rd and 7th are 'flattened'.)

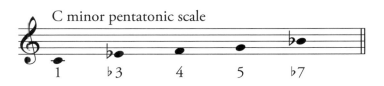

The Blues scale – this contains the flattened 3rd, 5th and 7th – these are also known as 'blue' notes. The scale consists of the root, flattened 3rd, 4th, flattened 5th, natural 5th and flattened 7th.

Composer's notes – What's in the Bag?

Style & History

'What's in the Bag?' is written in a funk style. Funk was developed by African-American musicians, who infused soul, jazz and R&B into a new type of dance music. Funk songs often have long sections of just one chord, with riffs (short musical ideas) played over the top. Getting the articulation correct for this style of tune is crucial for a convincing performance.

Listen to **James Brown**'s 'Get Up' or 'Papa's got a Brand New Bag' – excellent examples of this genre. Also have a listen to the **Miles Davis** tune 'So What' and you may notice some rhythmic similarities with this first tune.

Harmony

At the solo section (letter H), take the approach of a long, slow build up over 16 bars. Initially, play in between the backing figures that you can hear on the backing track. Any of the riffs used for the head can be used anywhere in the solo section. Construct your own riffs using the pentatonic scale below:

As well as the pentatonic, a blue note can be occasionally introduced. But don't hold it for a long duration – use it as a 'passing' note to a 'safe' chord note (i.e. the root, 3rd, 5th or 7th of the chord).

Rhythm

At letters C and F there is a counter melody on the backing track, don't let this throw you. Play riff 2 with plenty of confidence.

Tips & Projects

To get the correct style for this tune, you will need to pay particular attention to the articulations. In general, play this piece strongly, more so when the note has an accent marked. Many of the notes have staccato or tenuto marks indicated, this is where the real funkiness comes from. If you have a look through the tune you'll notice that there are very few notes without some sort of articulation.

If you find it difficult to achieve all of the articulations and play the right notes, make it easier for yourself: play the sections at letter A, B and C on one note, concentrating on just the articulation. Then, once you're happy, add the pitches back in.

What's in the Bag?

Rob Hughes and Paul Harvey

Free to Solo: Flute/Violin

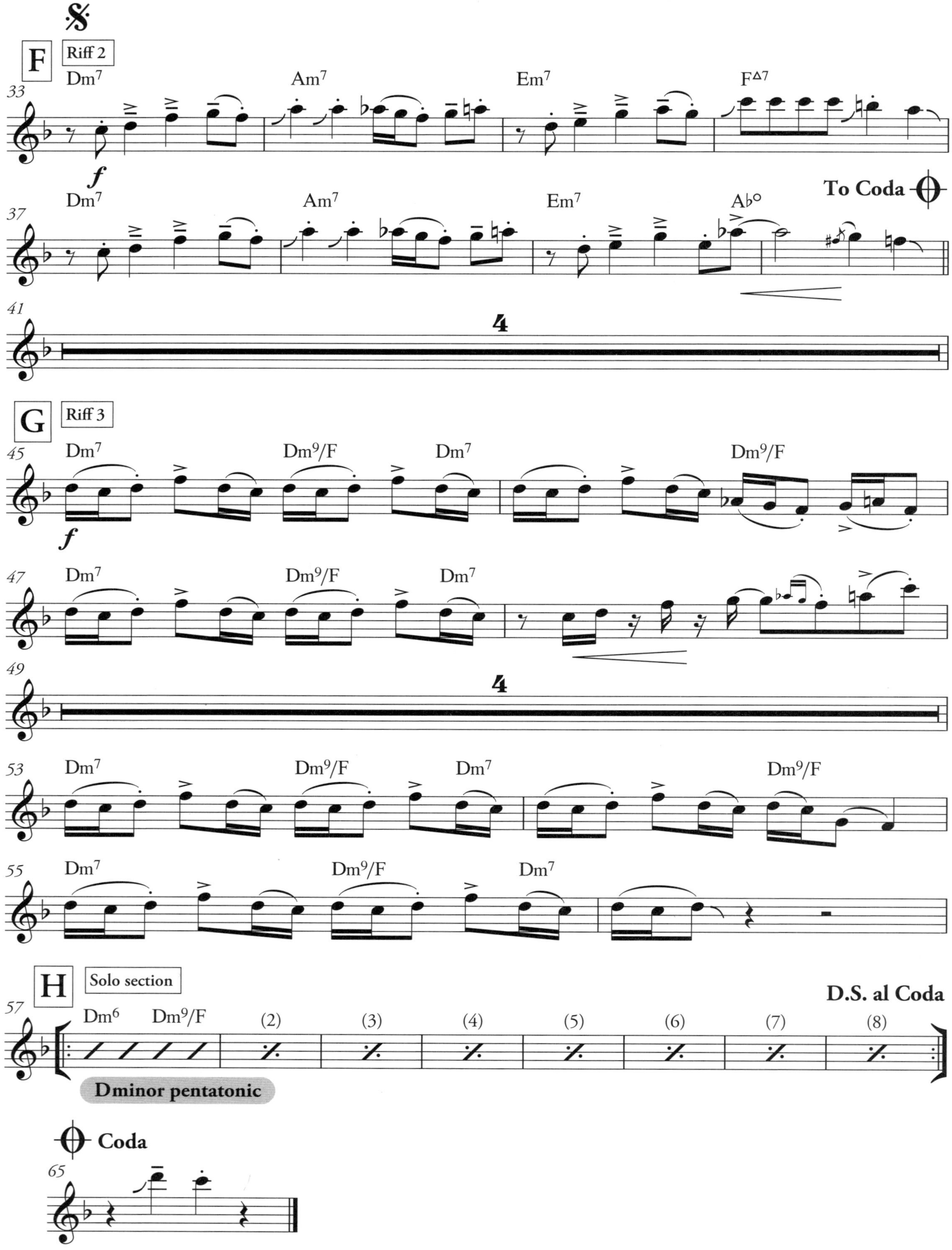

Composer's notes – Taylor Made

Style & History

'Taylor Made' is a gentle folk tune with a simple melody and chord structure. Have a listen to **Paul Simon**'s 'Bridge Over Troubled Water', **Bob Dylan**'s 'Blowin' in the Wind' or **James Taylor**'s 'Carolina in My Mind' to get an idea of the modern folk style.

Harmony

The scale below can be used for soloing in this tune. Play the scale then sing the scale, then play it again! This will help you to get in touch with the notes you will be using. Make use of the blue note now and again for a touch of 'spice' if you like.

The circled notes are the 'stronger' notes of the scale – they are the notes that make up the chord relevant to this scale. If you want your solo to sound 'safe' and 'grounded' use these notes, if you want it to sound a little more distant from the chords, try using the notes that are not circled.

Rhythm

The rhythm below may seem tricky; listen to the demo track whilst looking at the part. This way you will start to associate how this rhythm looks on paper with what you can hear.

Tips & Projects

As 'Taylor Made' has a reflective quality, it would make musical sense to leave plenty of space within your solo. Below are the chords for letter E, try adding these suggested notes:

These notes are, again, the stronger notes of each chord. They are the roots and 3rds. If this seems tricky, to begin with you can use the tune again (from letter C).

The backing track fades out towards the end so try to match this in your playing by getting softer and using more space.

Taylor Made

Rob Hughes and Paul Harvey

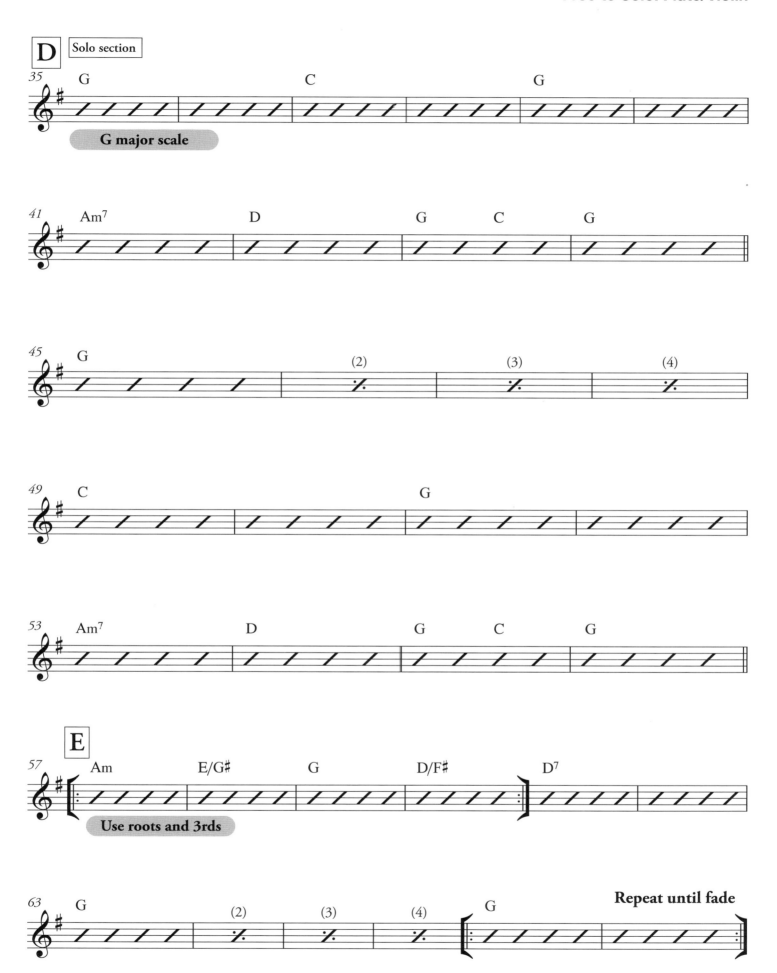

Composer's notes – Detroit Cowboy

Style & History

'Detroit Cowboy' is a Motown-style tune. Motown was a record label started by **Berry Gordy**, **Jr**. in Detroit and was sometimes referred to as the 'hits factory'. They had a winning pool of musicians and writers who contributed to the majority of the songs.

The Motown sound consisted of prominent and interesting bass lines and the use of call-and-response type melodies. Brass and string sections were also important, as was the use of the tambourine.

Some of the numerous Motown artists include: **Mary Wells**, **The Supremes**, **The Four Tops**, **The Jackson 5**, **Boyz II Men** and **The Commodores**. Listen to **The Temptations** tune 'Ain't Too Proud to Beg' to get a flavour of the classic Motown sound.

Harmony

You can use the major scale and blue note below to solo with in this tune.

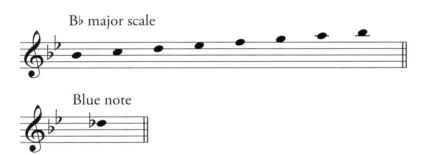

Rhythm

This next rhythm looks worse than it actually is. Put simply, the tied notes add up to a crotchet but are not played on the beat. The best way to work on this rhythm is to look at the part whilst listening to the demo track. Do this a few times and you will soon get used to how to play this phrase.

Tips & Projects

'Detroit Cowboy' has a 16-bar solo at letter D. It can be difficult to solo for a set amount of bars and then return back to the tune at the correct time (letter E). To begin with, don't improvise the first time you get to letter D, instead count the 16 bars and listen out for clues on the backing track as to where you need to come back in.

When you do solo over this section, it should then be second nature to you when the 16 bars are up.

The solo section at letter G is a chance to really go for it. You do not need to worry about coming back in as the tune doesn't return.

Detroit Cowboy

Rob Hughes and Paul Harvey

Composer's notes – Musique Rom

Style & History

'Musique Rom' is a jazz tune and, as it's in 3 time, could be referred to as a 'jazz waltz'. The head is a straightforward melody that can be played as written, perhaps with a lightly decorated (ad lib.) version on the Dal Segno.

Another example of a jazz waltz is 'My Favourite Things' by **Rodgers** and **Hammerstein**. This featured in the musical *The Sound of Music* and has become a firm favourite for many jazz musicians over the years.

Harmony

Below is a pentatonic scale which can be used for the entire solo. To add interest and tension, try adding in the blue note below. Remember to pass from this note to a 'safe', main chord note quickly.

Bb major pentatonic scale

Blue note

Rhythm

In your solo, borrow some of the different rhythmic ideas from the head such as bars 5, 13 and 27. This will give your solo a sense of coherence. You can use them as they are, or develop them by perhaps swapping the order of the pitches, or maybe omitting a rest or two.

Tips & Projects

After working on the pentatonic scale above, use the following as a suggestion for the solo section:

This example is for the first chord in the solo section. It outlines the most important notes of the chord: the root, 3rd and 7th.

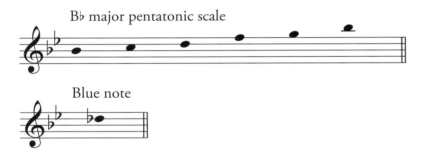

Bb△7

Below are the notes to use over the second chord in the solo. Again it's the root, 3rd and 7th of the chord. Practise playing these chord notes with the backing track. Once you can achieve this with ease, play the notes in a different order. Next, alternate between using the pentatonic scale and these chord notes.

Fm7

Musique Rom

Rob Hughes

Composer's notes – Funk 24

Style & History

'Funk 24', as the title suggests, is a funk tune! The background to this genre is described in the text for 'What's in the Bag?' on page 4. One band who are synonymous with funk are **The Average White Band**. If you listen to one of their most famous tracks, 'Pick Up The Pieces', you may hear some of the influences that 'Funk 24' has drawn on. To really get into the funky style, pay particular attention to the written dynamics and articulations.

Harmony

Use the pentatonic scale below for improvising, any of these notes will work well in your solo. Start your solo with a sense of space, don't try to cram in all the notes at once otherwise you will have nothing left to play towards the end. Think about the solo as a conversation – when you meet someone you don't normally speak at 100 mph, so apply this rationale to your solo.

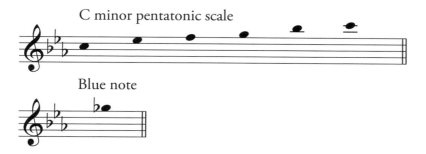

Rhythm

This piece has lots of funky rhythms. Develop your own riffs based on the rhythm of the first four bars, shown below. For example, start by playing the riff a few times until you have memorized it, then copy the rhythms but change two or three of the pitches.

Once you have mastered this, alter one or two of the rhythms so that you are gradually moving away from the original idea. This is a great way to start a progression that you can build on through your solo.

Tips & Projects

Work out how to play the 8-bar solo which starts at bar 17 (demonstrated on the CD). Once you can play it from memory, have a go at writing it out.

Funk 24

Rob Hughes and Paul Harvey

Composer's notes – Hold On

Style & History

'Hold On' is composed in the 'Philly Soul' style. Philly (or Philadelphia) Soul, has funk and jazz influences, often with elaborate instrumental arrangements. Those well known for this style include: **McFadden** and **Whitehead** ('Ain't No Stoppin' Us Now'), **Jackie Wilson**, **The Three Degrees** and **Grover Washington, Jr**.

This is a ballad, so be sure to work on being expressive with your dynamics – this will help to get across the melodic intentions of the tune. Play with confidence, but not too loudly.

Harmony

If you make your first eight bars spacious, the solo will have time to build up gently. The main scale to solo with is shown below, together with a blue note.

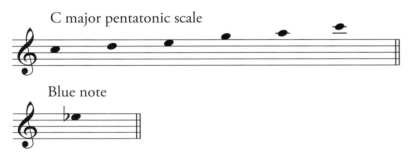

Once you are comfortable with the pentatonic scale, look at the chord changes at bars 45 and 47. The chord is shifting from major to minor and it would also be favourable to include the major 7th going to the minor 6th. Here are the strong chord notes:

Rhythm

At letter D there is a rhythm indicated in the part, if you included or referenced it in your improvisation it will sound great! Solo for the first eight bars then play what is written at letter D for three bars. Then try using just the rhythm from letter D, but changing the pitches to whatever you prefer.

Tips & Projects

This tune uses 'acciaccaturas' throughout to achieve a soulful vibe. They are brief in duration, played as though 'brushed' on the way to the principal note (which receives virtually all of its notated length).

They are also sometimes described as 'crushed' notes, which may help you in tackling this type of ornament. Have a go at writing a 4-bar phrase using an acciaccatura at least once.

Hold On

Rob Hughes and Paul Harvey

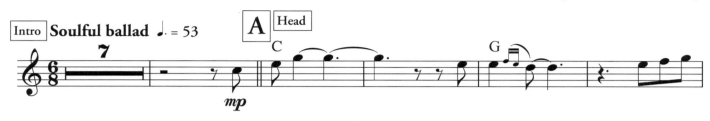

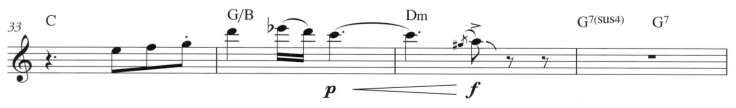

Composer's notes – Mystery

Style & History

'Mystery' is a reggae tune. Reggae is a music genre that originated from Jamaica in the late 1960s. Two strong rhythmic devices are often used with this style of music: the second and fourth beats of each bar are usually accented (as played by the guitar chords on this track) and the bass often leaves the first beat of the bar silent or tied over from the previous bar. Harmonically, the music is usually very simple, sometimes the entire song will have no more than one or two chords. These simple repetitive devices add to reggae's sometimes-hypnotic effect. Listen to 'I Shot the Sheriff' by **Bob Marley** or 'Red Red Wine' by **UB40** for examples of great reggae tunes.

Harmony

It's worth noting that this piece shifts between minor sections, letters A, C, D and F, and major sections, letters B, E, G and H.

The blues scale below can be used for soloing.

Rhythm

We have several crotchet triplets in this tune; this involves playing three crotchets in the time of two. A common mistake is to rush the last crotchet, so make sure that they are all even and laid back, which will fit in with the easy-going reggae character. Listen carefully to the demo track to get the idea.

Tips & Projects

The feel of the piece is quite relaxed, so convey this by letting your solo be open, unhurried and spacious. As a starting point, take some quotes (short melodic ideas) from the tune itself.

At letter F you can hear the organ playing simple phrases on the backing track – as an exercise, try copying or answering them.

On the repeat of letter G the backings come in again – work on playing around them at first (play in between the phrases) until your solo becomes more intense, at which point you may decide that you want to play over them.

Mystery

Rob Hughes and Paul Harvey

Composer's notes – Busticate

Style & History

'Busticate' is quasi-orchestral with a repetitive, rhythmic accompaniment and an angular melody. One of the best exponents of this type of music is **Mike Mower** – a British-based saxophonist and composer who has written for the saxophone group **Itchy Fingers**. This genre bridges the gap between jazz and classical music.

Harmony

The solo section starts at letter C, where you can use the pentatonic scale below. Add in the blue note for colour.

F minor pentatonic scale

Blue note

At letter D the chord sequence changes. You can still use the pentatonic scale but at bar 40, use the arpeggio below.

Practise this without any backing at first – play three bars of the pentatonic scale and then one bar of the arpeggio.

Db major arpeggio

At letter E the chord sequence changes again. Use the pentatonic scale for the first two bars of letter E.

At bar 43, try using the major 7th arpeggio (below).

Eb major 7th arpeggio

Rhythm

Perhaps the trickiest aspect of this tune is rhythm. To accomplish this you will need to be rhythmically very strict with yourself and have a 'rock solid' inner pulse – you must always know where beat one is!

Tips & Projects

Here's an example of a 'blue note in action'. Come up with some variations, and include them in your solo.

Busticate

Rob Hughes

Composer's notes – Nital

Style & History

'Nital' is written in a Latin-jazz style (a general term given to jazz music with Latin-American rhythmic influences). In comparison with traditional jazz, Latin jazz uses straight quavers, rather than swung.

To get acquainted with the sound, listen to 'The Girl from Ipanema', a well-known Latin tune. Play 'Nital' with a gentle volume, save your more energetic playing for the end of the piece.

Harmony

Use this pentatonic scale and blue note at letter D:

At bar 45 we have a diminished chord, this features a flattened 3rd and 5th, and a diminished 7th.

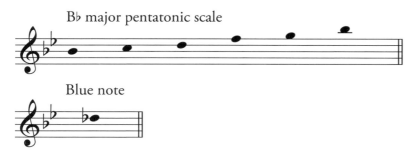

At letter G, use the pentatonic scale again, when you get to bar 85 change to the major scale below:

For bars 95–96 use an E♭ major arpeggio.

Rhythm

Play the rhythm shown here (from bar 20) with the same vigour as the guitar displays on the backing track from bar 32. Your playing needs to be very tight and crisp.

Tips & Projects

Write out a solo for the first four bars of letter D. If possible, incorporate the arpeggio idea from the harmony section at bar 45. As this is the start of your solo, make sure it's not too busy.

Nital

Rob Hughes and Paul Harvey

Track Listing

1. What's in the Bag?
2. Taylor Made
3. Detroit Cowboy
4. Musique Rom
5. Funk 24
6. Hold On
7. Mystery
8. Busticate
9. Nital

Tracks 4 and 8 written by Rob Hughes, all other tracks written by Rob Hughes and Paul Harvey.

As an additional bonus, you will find MP3 demonstration versions for all the other instruments in this series (see below for accessing MP3s). These can be used to further your appreciation of how different musicians, on a variety of instruments, approach the same improvisational material.

Recording Acknowledgments

Soloists (demo tracks):

Alto sax, Flute and Tenor sax – **Rob Hughes**

Clarinet – **Richard Beesley**

Guitar – **Paul Harvey**

Trombone – **Barnaby Dickinson**

Trumpet – **Graeme Flowers**

Violin – **Chris Haigh**

Backing tracks:

Alto sax, Bass Clarinet, Clarinet, Flute, Soprano sax and Tenor sax – **Rob Hughes**

Guitars, Bass and all programming – **Paul Harvey**

Recorded and mixed by **Rob Hughes** and **Paul Harvey** at Pocket Studios, June-October 2010

Using the CD

On the enclosed CD you will find demonstration versions of each tune, with the instrumental line played in full, as well as backing tracks for you to play along with.

Insert the 'Free to Solo' CD – the backing tracks should appear after a few moments and can either be played or imported, as you would with any other audio CD.

Accessing the CD backing tracks:

The backing tracks are regular CD audio tracks. If used with a *conventional CD player*, only the backing tracks will play.

To play the backing tracks *on a computer*, first open a media player such as iTunes or Windows media player.

Accessing the MP3 demonstration tracks:

Insert the 'Free to Solo' CD into a computer, navigate to your CD drive and click open. Find the folder marked 'MP3 demos'. Inside the folder you will find a folder for your instrument, you can then copy these demonstration versions to your computer's media player.